ANTIQUE or *Shabby Chic?*
Appraise & Sell Like a Pro!

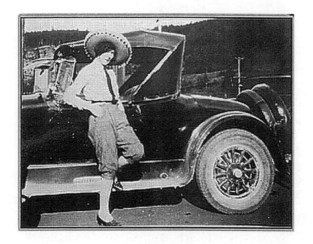

by

Leslie Goodwin

Amazon Kindle BEST SELLER!

NOTES AND DISCLAIMERS

Leslie A. Goodwin

**Also available as an eBook on Amazon.com
and Barnes & Noble.com**

CONTACT

Contact me at Incatrader@comcast.net to order another copy or electronic copy, to be on mailing list for updates or for my future books.

ACKNOWLEDGEMENTS

I'm grateful to Kathy Dieterich, Diana Hornby and Janis Rapoport de Miranda for patient editing and title crunching.

Thanks also to Judy Fisher, David Levin and Linda Parnes. Mary Jackson went beyond the call of duty to give me an antique dealer's viewpoint. THANK YOU to everyone else who encouraged me. If you like this book, please leave a glowing review and spread the word! Lg

PHOTO CREDITS

Cover design and **photos** are by Leslie Goodwin
except for the vintage photos, which are by unknown
photographers. Don't forget to identify your family
photos. LG

Table of Contents

Leslie Goodwin

NOTES

INTRODUCTION

Grammy's attic was overflowing. Now it's all yours. What now? Maybe you want to buy storage lockers or sell your thrift shop bargains. How do you get top dollar for that rare rocker? How do you know what to keep and what to toss?

You want to cash in on your stash. *But first you need to know:*

WHAT IS IT? *Should you toss it, keep it, or sell it?*

WHAT'S IT WORTH? *How to search like the pros. Find the value in seconds without spending a dime!*

HOW TO SELL IT: *Get paid what it's worth. More than 8 ways to sell online or off.*

I'll show you how to appraise or sell your goods, using the same methods antiques dealers use every day. I'll share tips, tricks, and trade secrets to bring you up to speed in minutes.

This book will pay for itself a hundred times over! **Here is your own personal guide to all internet and other essential resources.**

ABOUT ME

I bought my first antiques in 1967 in a flea market in Mexico but I have been a professional antiques dealer for 20 years. I've sold on eBay since 1998, selling more than 500 items there and hundreds on Craigslist.

The most expensive item I ever sold on eBay went for $22,854.

The most expensive item I have ever marketed privately sold for $54,000

I was an appraiser on the very first U.S. *Antiques Roadshow* in Denver. Before I started trading full time, I worked as a journalist and magazine editor. I've sold everywhere from flea markets to prestigious antique shows. I am also a professional art restorer.

Part of my folk art collection is on display at the International Folk Art Museum in Santa Fe, NM. through October 2012.

Now I want to share my secrets with you. I can help you identify and market your treasures like a pro with little or no investment. *Ready? Let's get started on a mammoth treasure hunt!*

WHAT IS IT?

It isn't always obvious.

Don't sell anything of historical significance to your family. Record all information on reverse side.

WHAT IS IT?

When it's time to clean out Mom and Dad's home, or have a garage sale, there are usually some antiques, some true treasures, some vintage furniture, and lots of plain old trash to sort through.

Dad was a pack rat. Mom could never get him to part with anything. He had some pretty unusual *junque* as he liked to call it. *Where do you begin? How do you separate the trash from the treasure?*

TOSS IT, KEEP IT, OR SELL IT? First ask: Does it have sentimental value? You might be able to get 100 bucks for Grandma Tootie's cookie jar but you can't put a price on memories. If it reminds you of the love she baked into each delicious Snickerdoodle each time you look at the jar, keep it to hand down.

Family photos should stay in the family. Only discard those which are ruined beyond use. Share the duplicates.

Write lightly and **only in pencil** on the back of each, any info you know including date. Someone in your family may someday research genealogy.

The next step is figuring out what you have. *It isn't always obvious.* A humble little can could be a valuable rare advertising tin and that graceful antique vase could be a modern imposter worth a pittance!

First start a list. You'll need an accurate description and condition report for each item.

The quickest, low-tech way to figure out what you've got is to get a little help. If you have a friend who deals in antiques and collectibles, offer to pay for help. *Not to sell, Not to appraise. Just to name it.*

MARKS TELL THE TALE: Make note of all marks. They are the clues to identifying age, maker, and even country of origin.

Some antique dealers won't mind helping you identify your stuff if there's something in it for them. Viola Fairshake is a local consignment store owner known for her honesty. She may be willing to help out if you consider consigning to her later on.

But another kind of dealer, we'll call Joey "The Nose" is known for his ability to sniff out estates ripe for the picking. He can rip through a house like a hungry shark at a surfer beach.

And Barry Goodbuyer advertises everywhere. He's always buying. But *he won't even look* at your stuff unless it's for sale...and *you name the price.*

It's a conflict of interest for dealers to appraise *and* buy from you. They need to buy well and sell for a profit and their time is valuable.

You won't call a dealer usually until you're ready to sell. After you know what you have and what it's worth, you can call a dealer to sell.

Don't expect a friend *or* dealer to identify (or appraise) your items for free. Even if it's just beer and pizza, pay something.

This is not meant to imply that antiques dealers like to drink, however, beer/pizza is the universal currency when friends help friends and dealers are often hungry!

IS IT MARKED? Grab the list: Does it have a maker's mark? Patent mark? Anything written anywhere?

Record all marks on your list. US patent marks were first issued in 1836 (see BOOKMARKS at end). Canadian patent dates start in 1869.

You can research the age via patent mark. However, it doesn't always mean the item dates to patent date. It only tells *the first year it was patented.* So if it has an 1836 mark, it can't be older than that.

What now? Go to the library to look up the marks? Price guidebooks such as Schroeder's, or Kovel's are found at most every public library and online. They're useful for the pictures and descriptions. *I recommend searching online, though, for updated pricing.*

In the next chapter, I'll show you the best ways to research online.

First, here's everything you ever wanted to know about silver marks.

Silver Marks and What They Mean

Sterling, 925, Esterlina or Plata (Spanish for sterling and silver) are all 925 parts silver out of 1000; the rest usually is copper.

800 means it is 800 parts silver. German stuff is often marked 800. Some old Mexican stuff is sometimes marked **980.**

COIN or PURE COIN (usually seen in capital letters) means coin silver—usually about 900 parts. Early American silver workers crafted from melted coins and marked their items COIN or PURE COIN or 900.

EPNS means electroplated nickel silver plated. Plated means covered with a thin coating of silver.

Triple Plate or Quadruple Plate means silver plated with three or four coats.

Copper Over Silver means silver plated.

Silver Soldered means silver plated.

German Silver, **Nickel Silver, Alpaca or Alpacca /Alpakka** all have no silver. They are alloys of copper, nickel, and zinc.

Sheffield Silver is silver plated.

Bullion or Fine Silver is 999 parts silver and is the standard referred to as spot price.

Old British Silver Marks don't use numbers for silver content. They have little pictures of lions and such.

Anything you can't identify can be searched on sites listed in BOOKMARKS (at end of book)or in any silver marks book. If you buy much silver, invest in a silver marks book.

GOOD SILVER ISN'T ALWAYS MARKED: Old handmade jewelry especially Navajo and other tribal jewelry is often unmarked. Some Spanish colonial silver such as, pre-1820s silver from Peru and Bolivia was rarely marked with silver content. For more on this check out my website. Address is in BOOKMARKS at end of the book.

SELLING SILVER FOR SCRAP: With precious metal prices so high recently, many of us are selling unwanted silver items to scrap buyers. They pay according to spot price—the price you see quoted in the paper or online. It constantly fluctuates, based on commodity selling per troy ounce of fine (999) silver. A troy ounce equals 1.1 regular ounces.

Most scrap buyers pay 50-75% of spot price (more if you're lucky or sell a large quantity). They deduct the difference between what you have and pure silver.

If you have unmarked silver, they will test it with acids to determine the silver content and pay you accordingly.

You can't sell silver plated items to be melted down.

Gold items will be marked with purity grades 10K, 14K etc. The higher the number, the more gold. If not marked with K marks, it is plated, filled, or another metal. If it's tarnished, it's not gold. High purity gold doesn't tarnish.

Silver has **two values.** One is the weight and the other is antique value. By weight, if you have a sterling spoon that weighs one troy ounce (1.1 regular ounces), the scrap buyer will pay you 92.5 % of the spot price and then take 50% off that. Remember, sterling is 925 parts silver.

Let's say the spot price is $35. per troy ounce. He would pay you $16.19 if you sell it for melt ($32.37 is 92.5% of $35 minus $16.18 (50%). If your buyer pays 75%, you net $24.27 for your spoon.

You can also sell scrap silver and gold to a jeweler. They may pay more because otherwise they have to pay retail to buy metals to make their jewelry. If you know a silversmith who casts silver, he or she may be a good buyer for your silver.

True antique silver items have both weight value and antique value. Collectors love antique Gorham silver, for example. If you think you may have some good, old hand-made Native American Indian jewelry, don't sell it for melt.

So research the value, compare it to the going rate offered by silver scrap buyers and it's your call.

See the BOOKMARKS (last section) if you want to research silver marks and styles. If you suspect your jewelry or silver has artistic or antique value, don't sell it until you know more.

REAL RELIC or RUSTY REPRO? Because many antique and vintage items have been reproduced, it can be difficult to tell if yours is the real McCoy or a clever copy.

There are many books about fakes and reproduction antiques. You may want to read some of them. Meanwhile, here are some shortcuts for detecting modern copies.

GOOGLE IT: Recently someone wrote asking me to appraise her poster by a famous artist. She'd seen one on that famous TV show and was hoping hers was equally rare.

A quick Google search turned up 1,000 images of the same poster. It has been widely copied but few of the original printing survived. The chances that it was original were not good.

So what can we conclude? If you see thousands of items exactly like your rare antique on the internet, chances are it is a reprint, reproduction or copy. And yes, her poster was new.

Here's a commonly misrepresented object. The "Spanish colonial" painting shown is a brand new replica sold as old. I bought it in Peru from a vendor who had dozens like it in all shapes and sizes and subject matter. Both front and back are "antiqued" with brown stain.

Spanish colonial? Not hardly.
It was painted last month.

You can find hundreds like it for sale when Googling, yet unsuspecting buyers are paying through the nose for them every day thinking they are buying actual antiques.

I discuss these paintings and several other new items often sold as old in my website. Google *Fake or Fabulous* and it is the first page that comes up.

Once you search for your item online, read online guides or ask experts, you'll soon be able to tell the rusty repro from the real relic.

CRASH COURSE IN COPIES: Here's a list of the most commonly copied antiques:

Cast iron toys (with Phillips head screws. Almost every one you see is new), tin advertising signs, Tiffany style lamps, old master paintings, Audubon and Currier and Ives prints, old posters, tin wind up toys, Mexican *retablo* paintings, carousel horses, glass paperweights, handmade quilts made in China, Fiesta pottery, Roseville pottery, Chippendale style furniture from Indonesia, Victorian style buggies from Indonesia, and old rocking horses. There are even "Navajo" rugs made in Pakistan.

If it's on this list, or you find thousands of the identical item in a search, your item may not be antique. Whip out your magnifying glass, Sherlock, and look for clues! What marks does it have? Where was it made? What's it made of?

MADE IN CHINA means it is NEW. Antique Chinese items won't be marked Made in China. If it's marked Made in U.S.A., or better yet, Made in United States of America, it's most likely pre—1960.

If it's made of plywood, it's newer. If it has Phillips head screws, it is most likely new (or repaired.) If it is made out of aluminum it was made after 1889.

NOTES

WHAT'S IT WORTH?

Wholesale or retail?

NOTES

WHAT'S IT WORTH?

Wholesale or retail? Your items have two values: wholesale and retail. The wholesale price is usually about half of retail.

Dealers pay wholesale and try to sell at retail. If they pay $10. they want to sell for at least $20.

The $10. markup is their salary for marketing the goods to a retail buyer. A retail buyer is not buying to resell and therefore can afford to pay more.

HIRE AN APPRAISER or *DO IT YOURSELF?*

How are you going to find the value of your goods? You could...

- **Pay someone like Viola Fairshake** or a knowledgeable friend who isn't buying from you.

- **Pay a professional appraiser** at hourly rates between $50 and $500 an hour. Not all appraisers are accredited and they all have specialties.

- **Use an online appraisal service** (Find them by Googling. You email photos and pay by the item.)

- **Appraise your own items** *for no investment except your time.*

I will teach you how to use some of the very same tools that professionals use everyday to save money and time. It's not hard. It's fun and with a little practice, takes just a few minutes per item. If you are appraising for insurance, though, you may need to hire a certified appraiser.

USING eBAY TO PRICE

You'll see Barry Goodbuyer frantically tapping away on his laptop at the auction or thrift shop. He's checking pricing online--mostly on eBay or by Googling.

Internet searches are the easy, cheap way to find current values. We don't care what prices sellers are currently asking, though. We want to know what has sold and for how much.

Here's how to search like a pro:

1. Go to **www.eBay.com**. Find a green button marked **SEARCH** at the top of the page.

2. Click on the **advanced** button next to it.

3. On this screen, where it says "**enter key words or item number**" type in the name of your item (clown cookie jar, for example).

4. Click "**completed listings.**"

5. Click the dark blue **SEARCH** button.

A page comes up showing every similar item listed in the last 30 days. The ones marked SOLD are the *only* ones that sold.

CONGRATULATIONS! You are now an expert at searching completed listings on eBay! The prices of thousands of items are at your fingertips. eBay pricing tends to be whole-sale, though.

Most items show up for sale on eBay within a 30 day period. If at first you can't find it, try describing it differently: *clown pottery bowl, clown canister, McCoy pottery jar.*

Internet searches are an important tool professional antique dealers use to price. eBay is only the beginning.

Now I'll introduce you to some of my other favorite research sites.

MORE GREAT SEARCH SITES

Search on Google and you'll find thousands of online resources. Just go to Google.com and type in the name of the item. Google searches usually turn up everything for sale on earth.

Google Tip #1: If you choose the *images* option button, you'll see *images only* to help identify your items. This also works on Craigslist to view image thumbnails.

Google Tip #2: In Google search results, you will see a reference and the highlighted word *cached.* **If you click on** *cached, i***t will take you to the very place in the website where you'll find it. Keep in mind that asking prices are meaningless.**

*Condition is everything when
valuing books. Having the original
dust jacket will boost value.*

Artfind.com is free to join and gives you access to lots of auction results for **fine art**. There's even an artist database.

Worthpoint.com and **Priceminer.com** archive old eBay and other auction results and charge for the info. You can join for between $10. and $50. a month and access eBay records — even those longer than 30 days.

MORE GREAT SEARCH SITES continued

AddALL.com for used books. It combines 16 book selling sites (doesn't include Amazon). Note these are asking prices only, no completed search available but good for researching editions and dust jackets etcetera.

Book value details: Condition determines the price of a book and an original dust jacket adds value.

If you want to buy or sell lots of books, you can even buy a scanner and application for your smart phone that allows you to scan the ISBN number of the book to instantly get prices from websites. Keep in mind, that any book published before 1970 won't have an ISBN number.

Google "book scouting software" to get software apps for automatically searching prices with your phone. There are also apps for scouting prices of everything on Amazon.com.

Pottery and Glass forum is a free online group. You join and then you can post photos of pottery and glass for members to help identify. Great for foreign, 1960s and art pottery. Potteryandglass.forumandco.com.

Replacements.com for China or Silver. They sell replacements for silverware and china patterns so you can identify by pattern. Also they sell retail, so you can sell to them and use it to find pricing as well.

MORE FREE APPRAISALS

Local Auctions: My favorite local auctioneer, "Speedy" Bidwell has been selling for 35 years and he's sold it all. His brain is a computer. He can estimate almost to the dollar the auction sale price of anything.

He is usually willing to give free informal estimates when I take him stuff to sell. Then I decide whether or not to consign to his auction.

Auctioneers will also sell on site at your house for a substantial lot. Attend your local auctions to get a feel for the market and get to know your local auctioneers.

Here's a true, funny story: My friend Fern (not her real name) is a picker. Nobody better. She can root out a ruby in a compost heap.

She called to say she'd found a cute 1930s highchair on sale half price at an estate sale—wooden, with red wheels that converts into a stroller.

"It's marked down to half," Fern said, "Fifty bucks. Should I buy it to sell?"

This time I said no. Two days before, at Speedy's Sunday auction, I had seen the same model sell for $2.50. Visit your local auction to get a feel for current values. You'll learn lots...*FAST!*

Local antique shows: You can see a lot of different goods at retail prices when you go to a show. You will learn from seeing how others market antiques and collectibles. You may even decide to sell at a show.

Here's a little-known fact: **Big auction houses** like Sotheby's, Skinner, Christie's and Heritage will look at photos and give *free auction estimates.*

The first three have a cast of experts you can email to inquire about your items for sale. High ticket items only. If you want to sell, they have to accept your item for auction.

For Heritage auctions, there is even an online evaluation form. Here's the list of items Heritage *doesn't* sell: **commercial figurines (e.g. Hummell, Lladro), posters of art, post-war Asian objects, reproductions, paintings on velvet.** Check out the the big auctions online to see if they sell any items like yours. Before contacting, identify the expert in charge (such as fine art, American Indian art, glassware, silver. **(For links to each site, see BOOKMARKS at end).**

VALUING FINE ART: TIPS

Volumes have been written about this weighty topic. I can't tell you in a few words how to authenticate signatures, how to distinguish an original from a print etcetera but following are a few quick tips.

- Fine art that isn't signed is much less valuable than signed art.

- Research artist signatures on Askart.com, Artfind.com and see BOOKMARKS at end for more guides.

- A famous reference book titled *Davenport's Art Reference and Price Guide* is also helpful but expensive to buy. You might find it at the library. When you hear an artist is "listed", it means the artist is listed here and in other books and online sites.

- Limited Editions: If there's a mark that looks like pencil that says for example; 100/250, it is a limited edition. The total number printed was 250 and this is number 100. It is not original art.

Prints on canvas: If the paint on the edges of that "oil" painting ends in an even, straight line, you most likely own a giclée print. A copy printed on canvas. It can look an awful lot like an original painting...sometimes they paint clear texture over the top to look like brush strokes.

The *provenance* can be helpful in identifying fine art. Provenance means the history of ownership.

Family legends and provenance can be misleading. Great Aunt Trudy was born in 1900 but she also bought tchochtkes on the shopping channel. Not everything in her house is antique. Some of it dates to the 1980s. You will have some good news and some bad while searching and appraising. Try not to take it personally.

When Uncle Igor's legendary copy of *War and Peace* you thought was the valuable first edition turns out to be the 1949 Book Club Edition selling currently for $1.99, take it in stride and congratulate yourself on your new searching skills

Final note about informal appraisals: Not all appraisals are acceptable for insurance. Consult your agent if you want to insure your antiques against loss or damage. Hire a professional, certified appraiser if you want to insure your items.

Maude before and after. Don't try to fix artwork on your own.

CONSERVATION TIPS: Fix it or forget it? Generally speaking, you should offer for sale in as-is condition. **Don't re-glue, retouch or refinish.** *Use a soft brush to dust the surfaces of artwork, sculptures and books. Then stop.*

Some old furniture can lose value when refinished. Leave your old furniture alone. When in doubt, don't touch it. Keep all the loose or broken pieces together with the object so it can be reassembled later.

Fine art such as paintings, drawings and prints, however, will gain value by being professionally conserved. That big ol' hole and crumbly browned varnish is hurting the value of your painting. Resist the temptation to fix it yourself.

CONSERVATION TIPS continued

Art conservation or restoration is not for amateurs and you could destroy your art. But there are some simple fixes.

SIMPLE FIXES: If you see brown or yellowed paper behind a print or watercolor and on the edges where the mat rests, that is acid damage from the backing paper or mat. Left as is, the paper will continue to deteriorate until brown marks show on the face of the art.

With a modest investment, a framer can replace the mat with an acid-free mat and backing to save your art from further deterioration.

If it's Grandpa Bud's portrait or valuable collectible art, though, hire a pro to conserve it. Otherwise, if you offer it for sale, sell as-is and let the buyer deal with it. The photo of "Maude" is a painting I restored. **Dealers in your area can recommend a restorer. Don't be tempted to do- it-yourself.**

STORE LIKE A PRO: Always store artwork and furniture in a stable temperature environment, out of strong sunlight and high humidity or ultra low humidity.

Never store fine furniture, antiques or artwork in the garage or enclosed in plastic. They're just like us, they like to breathe and they like comfortable temperatures.

As an experiment, I rolled up a new, *unvarnished* painting on canvas and left it in the garage for a few winter months. When I unrolled it, it was cracked in a hundred places. *It was new, flexible and without cracks when I first stored it!*

Proper storage will protect art and antiques. Proper conservation will protect them from deterioration.

HOW DO YOU SELL IT?

Nine methods. Which is best?

NOTES

HOW DO YOU SELL IT?

Now that you've done your research, you're ready to price. You've done an online search and you know that Grandma's cookie jar is actually a rare and desirable McCoy crazy clown cookie jar. Several have recently sold on eBay for almost $200.

You've decided to sell, as everyone agrees, Grandma Tootie's cookies were horrible and that scary clown used to frighten you every time you went into the kitchen!

It's time to get some cash for your stash.

Here are nine ways to sell (not in any order), how to do it and the pros and cons of each:

1. **Sell to Local Dealer or Metal Dealer** for melt

2. **Craigslist, Etsy, Ruby Lane, Tias** or online service—not auctions, fixed price

3. **Online Auction** (eBay etcetera)

4. **Consign to a Big Auction House**

5. **Estate Sale** —hire a service

6. **Estate Sale or Garage Sale** —do it yourself

7. **Local Auction**

8. **Local Consignment Store or Rent a Flea Market Space**

9. **Classified Ads**

10. **Donate**

Next: How to sell and the pros and cons of each.

SELLING METHODS/ Pros and Cons

SELL TO A LOCAL DEALER

PRO: Instant pay, minimal hassle, no shipping or delivery. No added sales costs.

CON: Usually wholesale pricing. You must research each item for optimal pricing before selling.

LIST ON CRAIGSLIST

PRO: No cost to list, fast to list, easy to learn and do yourself, no shipping, instant cash pay. Can sell furniture or fragile items you wouldn't want to ship.

CON: Wholesale market, best for low- cost items, must meet with buyers. Items may take longer to sell and will have to be re-listed until they do.

SELL ON eBay

PRO: Do it yourself, commissions total about 13%. Exposure to international market, set your own price, set reserve, appropriate for most smaller items. OR you can hire someone to list for you on eBay for about 23%.

CON: Do it yourself. Time consuming. Learning curve. You have to ship or deliver, no good for large items, medium to slow pay. Must open a PayPal account to get payment.

INTERNET: RUBY LANE, ETSY, TIAS etc

PRO: You set price, low costs and commissions.

CON: Slow pay, must ship, learning curve to list, no guarantee of sale.

CONSIGN TO BIG AUCTION HOUSE/ Sotheby's, Christie's, Bonham and Butterfields etc.

PRO: Best chance to sell for top dollar, expert marketing help, authentication help and professional photography.

CON: High commissions, extra related costs, must ship. Item must be accepted by them. No guarantee of a sale. Slow to very slow pay.

ESTATE SALE done by others

PRO: All work of advertising, marketing is done for you. Items sell within a set time.

You get help valuing and sorting, you let the estate dealer run the sale. Fast pay.

CON: No control over pricing or discounting, possible theft, you must either provide the venue or haul everything to another location.

Commissions vary between 10 and 40%. You are trusting them to value items. Wear and tear to the home where you sell.

ESTATE OR GARAGE SALE do it yourself

PRO: Some minimal costs for advertising. Many items sell within a short time period, Cash sale. No commissions. You control pricing and make sales.

CON: You need an indoor venue. Garage sales have low prestige and draw lower prices. You do all the work or pricing, pay for advertising, work the sale, manage the money.

SALES METHODS Pros and Cons continued

LOCAL AUCTION

PRO: Fast pay, no upfront costs, no shipping, potential for retail sale. Commissions start at about 17.5%.

CON: Unpredictable results that could be wholesale. Highest end commissions to approx. 33%.

CONSIGNMENT STORE or FLEA MARKET SPACE

PRO: Retail sale. No shipping or selling. Marketing help and advice.

CON: Slow pay or no pay if item doesn't sell. Commissions equal difference between wholesale and retail.

CLASSIFIED ADS/Newspaper

PRO: You can market locally or nationally, see clients in your own time, control pricing and terms. No computer skills needed. Retail sale potential.

CON: Not practical for multiple items usually. Costs may be too high per item. May or may not draw potential buyers searching online.

DONATE

PRO: You get a tax deduction with receipt. Items may be dropped off or picked up. Fast recycling of unwanted items, hardly any work or trouble. Supports your favorite charity.

CON: No cash, just a tax deduction.

HOW TO SELL ONLINE

Sell on Craigslist: *The easiest way I know to sell online is on Craigslist.* CL is an online classifieds site. More than 50 million people use it in the U.S. alone and I'm a big fan.

One reason I like it? It's mostly FREE —unlike most sales sites. There are no costs to list or commissions to pay. Of all online sites, it's easiest to learn and use. Even a new user can list for sale in minutes. There are sites in most major U.S. and even foreign cities.

Here's how it works: You list items for sale, items wanted, or to trade, and buyers contact you directly either by email or phone (your choice).

It's not an auction. You set the terms. And meet with buyers. You don't ship if you don't want to. Selling out of town is discouraged for security reasons. You can ask for cash payment.

You can include up to four photos (or not) but photos will help you sell. So take photos with a digital camera and transfer them to your computer before listing. If you know some HTML, you can dress up your listings.

CL doesn't allow you to re-list daily or list in multiple locations at once and there are some restrictions on goods for sale. You can refresh your listing every 48 hours so it will come at the top of the search results.

Sell on eBay: To sell on eBay you must sign up as a user. You also have to sign up for a PayPal account to receive payment. At this writing, the two payment methods allowed by eBay are online or payment in person. You can't accept checks or money orders.

How does PayPal work? PayPal allows everyone to get paid via credit cards and more online. You can send to or receive money from anyone in the world who also has a PayPal account.

PAYPAL continued

With PayPal, you can use or accept credit cards, automatic withdrawal from a bank account or PayPal account or electronic checks.

Other online pay services are allowed, but most buyers use PayPal. The money comes into your account. From there you can request a check mailed to you or request an automatic withdrawal to your bank account. If you want PayPal to mail you a check, there is a fee. It's all done in a few clicks of the mouse!

It costs 3% to pay with debit or credit card. It is free to send money if it comes directly from your bank account. It always costs to receive — about 3% —more if the money comes from abroad.

You have to sign up for a PayPal account to sell on eBay.

Is it safe? Yes, you have to register credit card and bank account information, but you're not alone. There are 94.4 million of users worldwide.

Once registered, go to the site and read the Safety links. Scumbags the world over will now try to learn your password through fake emails claiming to be from PayPal. **Don't give your password to anyone and don't answer any email that doesn't address you by your full registered name. The same goes for any correspondence from eBay.**

It's not the only game in town, but PayPal has become the standard for online commerce; a great way to accept credit card payments and it's fast.

When you sell on eBay, buyers pay for shipping. Sellers get paid by the buyer before they ship.

There are several choices for selling on eBay: at *auction, fixed price*, in an *eBay store* or *best offer*.

You can sell at *auction* or *fixed price* or you can have an eBay *online store*. In your eBay store, you sell for a fixed price.

With auctions, you can sell with or without **a reserve**. Auctions are for set time periods: 1, 3, 5, 7 or 10 days.

What is a reserve? It is the minimum auction sales price you will accept. If you sell at *no reserve*, then the highest bidder at the end of the auction is the winner. You can set the starting price anywhere you want.

Or you can set a *reserve*. If the bidding doesn't meet your reserve, your item doesn't sell and you can re-list it for a set time period.

If you sell at *Fixed Price*, then the first person to bid your price, gets the item. You can also give the option of *Best Offer*, wherein someone offers less and you can accept or not.

Fixed price listings are for 3, 5, 7, 10, or 30 day terms, or Good 'Til Canceled. Good 'Til Canceled renews automatically every 30 days until the item sells or you end the listing.

Or you can list your stuff in an **eBay store** where it will languish...er...*remain* until it sells, you un-list it, or the world comes to an end. Competition from other bidders and a deadline to commit seems to make buyers step up and bid at auction while they may procrastinate on a fixed price listing.

It takes patience to sell in an online store either on eBay, Ruby Lane, Etsy or any of the other online sites that aren't auctions.

After the sale, you package and ship. eBay charges you a commission on each sale and PayPal deducts a commission of about 3% when you receive money.

eBay changes its pricing frequently but generally speaking, you pay about 14% commission to sell on eBay which includes the PayPal commission. And consider your time invested, too.

You can list it yourself or get a trading assistant through eBay to list for you. If you click on the *Sell Item* link button, you will find the listing form. Yikes! It can be intimidating at first. At least you can click on HELP buttons throughout.

If you're prone to panic attacks, I recommend you get a savvy friend to show you the ropes or utilize eBay's help videos. OR when you click on the Sell Item button, click on *Sell it for me*, where you can find someone to list for you.

Like Craigslist, you will need digital photos of your item already stored on your computer and know where they are before proceeding. More advanced users can self—host their images. You can even donate a percentage of your sales to a choice of charities.

After the transaction, buyers can leave you feedback, grading you on the various aspects of the deal. You can also leave feedback, only you can't leave negative feedback. eBay made this policy change in 2008, denying sellers their fair right to report negative feedback on troublesome buyers. The moral of the story? Do your best to keep your buyers happy so they don't give you bad feedback.

Too much hassle? You can always pay someone to list your items on eBay. Most people charge around 23% of the item's asking price if you ship the item.

SELLING ONLINE—Non Auction Sites

There are other sites besides Craigslist where you sell online at a fixed price.

Some sites cater to antiques and collectibles, like Ruby Lane and TIAS. **Etsy** is geared toward artists who sell their own work and sellers of vintage items.

RubyLane.com is a site that caters to antiques, jewelry and collectibles. It's not an auction. You sell for a fixed price or accept offers.

I haven't personally used Ruby Lane, but I hear good things. They have recently announced a sister site called Ruby Plaza specifically to sell home decor, jewelry, fashion & accessories, and handcrafted items. It will be free to sell until 2012. Free is good!

Unlike eBay and CL, every Ruby Lane shop is prescreen-ed by an in-house team and must meet specific quality and professionalism standards before opening for business.

All open shops are required to follow an ongoing, stan-dard set of quality guidelines. There is a one-time setup fee of $75 per shop. This is refunded if your shop is not approved. After that, it costs 30 cents to list each item and there is a $20 monthly maintenance fee. You can pay your fees by personal check, money order or use PayPal.

TIAS.com features antiques and collectibles on the web. I have never used it to sell but my dealer friends speak well of it. Costs $39.99 a month for basic plan. Check it out if you want to do an online store.

Etsy.com allows you to sell handmade (by you), vintage or crafts supplies. They charge 20 cents for each item listed.

When you make a sale on Etsy, you will be charged 3.5% of the total sale price. This percentage does not include the shipping price.

SELLING ON ETSY continued

After four months if the item does not sell on Etsy, it is unlisted and you may easily re-list it if you like (at the same price).

SELL AT CONSIGNMENT STORE OR RENT FLEA MARKET BOOTH

Consignment/Antique Store: Viola Fairshake takes consignments in her store. You take the items to the store, she advises on pricing and sells for you, charging a commission but no rent.

It's a good option for furniture, used clothing or bulky items you don't want to ship or schlep around. If they don't sell after a set time, you have to pick them up.

Flea Market Booths/Spaces: Most U.S. cities have stores that rent spaces by the month where you set up a mini store. They usually charge rent plus commission. It is your job to stock, display, price and keep your little store tidy. They do the rest.

In my experience, it's a hard way to make a buck, but it does provide a place to warehouse a lot of items while they are for sale, and the staff does the selling for you, taking money, charging tax, accounting and giving you a check for proceeds (best case scenario!) at the end of the month.

If you dream of being a dealer, getting a booth is a good way to learn what sells and how to price in your local market.

You can also sell at an antique show or set up at a temporary flea market. They usually last one to three days.

You will need lots of merchandise to set up for an antique show and some of them have rules governing the age of items for sale. Don't forget an umbrella or canopy to sell outside in the summer.

At my first outdoor show, I had a patio umbrella but the heat was intense on the concrete in July. At 2 p.m., a lady collapsed of heat stroke in my booth! She got prompt medical attention. I kept on selling until closing because I'm a pro and because I was delirious and couldn't think straight any more.

LOCAL AUCTION HOUSE

You drop off items at the auction house. You get a check at the end of the day or usually within a week. Commissions whereI live vary between 17.5% to 33%.

If you have enough stuff, the auctioneer may be willing to come to your house and sell on-site. Some auctioneers let you set a reserve and others start the item at a reasonable amount and leave the rest to fate with no guarantees.

SELL AT BIG AUCTION HOUSE including Sotheby's, Skinner, Christies, Heritage, Bonhams and Butterfields, James D. Julia etc.

These are bricks and mortar auction houses that also sell from websites.

Big auction houses may be appropriate for selling high ticket items.

You've researched and you're still not sure if you have a high ticket item? Their specialists will tell you.

Just send digital photos via email to their specialists or the evaluation form for Heritage auction found on their website (See BOOKMARKS) and if they are interested in selling for you, they will give you an estimate.

Selling details: If you consign to Sotheby's you are responsible for all shipping, packing and insurance.

You will also pay a sales commission of approximately 20% plus photography and ticket fee if it doesn't meet reserve.

SALES METHODS/ Sotheby's continued

Sotheby's website explains: *The reserve is the confidential minimum selling price to which a consignor (you) and Sotheby's agree before the sale—your property's "floor" price, below which no bid will be accepted.*

If bidding on your item fails to reach the reserve, we will not sell the piece and will advise you of your options.

It is important to consider the reserve price in light of the fact that Sotheby's will assess fees and handling costs for unsold lots.

You will get paid about 40 days later. You must send your item at least 2 months before a sale.

If your item doesn't meet reserve, you will still pay expenses including shipping, insurance, photography, and handling costs.

Skinner auction standard commission rates for a seller are:

--10% for items selling for $7,500 or more;

--15% for items selling between $2,000 and $7,500

--20% for items selling for less than $2,000, with a minimum commission of $30 per lot.

Christies states on their website: *The consignor may also be charged for marketing, restoration, shipping, handling and other services.* For other auctions, see **BOOKMARKS.**

SALES METHODS SUMMARY

Fastest pay: Sell to a dealer, local auction, Craigslist, estate sale (do it yourself).

Medium pay: Estate sale, garage sale, eBay.

Slow pay: Big auction house, consignment shop, online (not auction).

Easiest: Donate, local auction, sell to dealer, consignment shop.

Biggest hassle: Big auction house, selling at flea market booth.

Medium hassle: Garage sale or estate sale (do- it- yourself), Craigslist, consignment shop, estate sale (someone does it for you). Newspaper ad.

Least hassle: Donate, sell to a dealer.

Retail sale: Big auction house, consignment shop, newspaper ad.

No commissions: Sell to dealer or on Craigslist. Newspaper ad.

Everyone wants to get retail for their goods. But as you can see, trying to get more money usually costs more time and money. Ultimately, you may decide to sell wholesale.

THE "ROADSHOW" FACTOR

The *Antiques Roadshow* has changed the way we look at antiques and collectibles--for better and worse. Thanks to the *Roadshow*, we all dream of treasure undiscovered in the attic we could sell to pay off the mortgage.

I appraised on the *Antiques Roadshow* when it first came to Denver. Here's the truth: We were told to appraise high for the camera as it makes better TV.

There were a dozen of us appraisers looking at thousands of items that day and only a few items were good enough to be filmed. In fact, only about *80 out of ten thousand items* brought to the *Roadshow* are filmed because they are truly extraordinary. That's why you didn't see me on camera.

I know, I know, we all want to get top dollar. It's just not always practical to hold out for top dollar if you factor in the costs and hassle involved and that intangible factor; the market.

Prices fluctuate depending on current collecting trends and the overall economy. Sometimes holding out means losing money. Sell if you want or need to, but do your homework first. If you don't need to sell, hold out for retail.

SUMMARY

- **Don't sell items of historical or sentimental value to your family.**
- **Don't expect dealer friends to appraise for free.**
- **Don't expect dealers to appraise.**
- **Do your own research.**
- **Set prices by recent completed sales, not by guide books or asking prices.**
- **Don't hold out for retail unless you have the time and expertise and are willing to pay extra costs.**
- **Don't sell to the first dealer you meet before doing your homework.**
- **Don't fix it yourself. Hire a pro if the item warrants it.**
- **Conserve and safely store the items you keep and enjoy for posterity.**

Now you know some tricks of the trade. You can find the current selling price of almost anything from your home computer.

Then if you decide to sell, you know the options and how to choose between them. You can research your family heirlooms and conserve them for generations to come. And who knows? You just might find that pot of gold hidden in the attic. If not, I know you'll have fun looking!

BOOKMARKS

Guide to the most useful internet sites and other resources.

BOOKMARKS

Here is a listing of all sites mentioned. This is not a comprehensive guide to buying and selling antiques and collectibles. These are my favorite resources:

RESEARCH AND APPRAISALS

Google.com is a great first search option. Try the IMAGES option to see only pictures.

eBay Video how to research completed listings: http://pages.ebay.com/sellerinformation/demo/researching.html

AddAll.com for used or antique books.

Amazon.com for newer books.

PriceMiner.com for past auction results from eBay, Goantiques, TIAS and other auction sites.

Http://www.priceminer.com/login/home.jsp

Worthpoint.com Past auction results from eBay. http://www.worthpoint.com/

Fake or Fabulous? Google Fake or Fabulous. My website will be the first in the list. It exposes items commonly misrepresented as Spanish Colonial in online sales.

http://home.comcast.net/~incatrader/index.htm

Pottery and glass forum: potteryandglass.forumandco.com

FINE ART RESEARCH

Findartinfo.com: Some free search by signature. http://www.findartinfo.com/

Bookmarks continued

Artfact.com for art. Artist database, auction results from hundreds of auction houses specializing in art results. Free, but you have to sign up for an account.

AskArt.com for online biographies of artists, image examples. You pay a fee for auction results.

Artistssignatures.com: examples of signatures. http://www.artistssignatures.com/index.php Moderate fees.

Artnet.com: European emphasis. Fees.

BIG AUCTION HOUSE FREE APPRAISALS

Christie's:

www.Christie's.com click on SERVICES link.

Heritage Auctions:

http://fineart.ha.com/common/contactus.php

Skinner Appraisal Services Department: 508-970-3299

Sotheby's Experts: for valuation of your items:

www.sothebys.com(click on Departments link)

Free appraisals from Sothebys: same site, click on Buy and Sell link

SELLING ONLINE

Craigslist: www.craigslist.org

Ebay: www.ebay.com

SELLING ONLINE continued

eBay Stores Help:
http://pages.ebay.com/storefronts/start.html

eBay Fees:
http://pages.ebay.com/help/sell/questions/sell-requirements.html

PayPal.com http://www.paypal.com/

RubyLane.com:
http://www.rubylane.com/info/aboutshops.html

TIAS: Online antiques collectibles sales site
http://www.tias.com/

Etsy.com : Online sales site for artists, craftsmen and sellers of vintage items.

SILVER MARKS / China Patterns

Silver Hallmarks: http://www.925-1000.com/

Replacements.com: Great resource for china patterns, silverware and holloware.

RESTORERS
Consult your local art or antiques dealer for a referral. Or email me.

U.S. PATENT NUMBERS BY DATE

Patent Dates by number. The age can vary plus or minus 20 years.
http://www.uspto.gov/patents/process/search/issu year.jsp

PLEASE CONTACT ME at Incatrader@comcast.net
to order another copy, or to order an electronic copy. Please write if you wish to be on the email list for updates, for my next book or if you have restoration work.

Thank you for buying my book and recommending it to your friends! Lg

Available in Electronic Digital Edition from Barnes & Noble.com and Amazon.com

NOTES

REINSTEIN

JUL 2 3 2012

Made in the USA
Lexington, KY
11 July 2012